METRO
MATURING EQUIPPING TRACK FOR REDEEMED ONES

G.A. THOMPSON

1

BELIEVER'S CATECHISM

Printed in the USA by Morris Publishing
3212 East Highway 30 Kearney, NE 68847
1-800-650-7888

First printing, January 2000
Second printing, 2002
Revised edition, April 2007

For more information, contact:
Sanctuary
3 Wexford Street
Needham Heights, MA 02494
1 800 647 0878
www.sanctuarybookstore.com

A Ministry of Jubilee Christian Church

ISBN Number 978-1-59704-001-3

I HEAR, AND I FORGET.

I SEE, AND I REMEMBER.

I DO, AND I UNDERSTAND.

INTRODUCTION

The Maturity Equipping Track for Redeemed Ones (METRO) will prepare you to do the most important work of ministry — bringing others to maturity and productivity.

Many come to Christ and are saved, but few reach the place of real spiritual maturity where they are able to reproduce themselves in others. Most are babies, still influenced negatively by the world, the flesh, and the devil and unable to do the work the Lord has commanded us to do.

Though the immediate goal of the METRO is to thoroughly ground you in the Faith, our ultimate goal is to create spiritual maturity and productivity in your life. We determine to equip you to disciple others. This equipping does not take place in a vacuum but in a covenant community. Community is necessary. Covenant community is another word for the kingdom of God. You must become kingdom conscious.

Jesus taught us to seek first the kingdom of God and His righteousness and that all other things we need will be added to us. The kingdom must become your priority. Jesus preached and taught the good news of the kingdom (Matthew 4:17). Paul preached and taught the good news of the kingdom (Acts 19:8; 28:23, 30-31). When you confessed Jesus Christ as the Lord of your life, you were born again to see and enter the kingdom (John 3:3-5). You are in God's kingdom right now (Colossians 1:13). To pray, "Your kingdom come, Your will be done" (Matthew 6:9) is to ask God to save men out of the kingdom of darkness (the rule of Satan) and bring them into the kingdom of light (the rule of Jesus Christ). The kingdom of God is a covenant community. God is calling you to live *in community and in covenant.* Community is the agreeing fellowship of at least three persons. Covenant is a spiritual contract or agreement binding believers to God by grace through faith and binding believers to each other as they walk in fellowship with God (1 John 1:7). You will never be lonely again.

The miracle of "community" does not just happen; it must be planned. God planned the community of the redeemed when He sent His Son to become a man in the earth. Jesus came to earth to build His church upon the truth of who He is — the Christ, the Son of the living God (Matthew 16:16). The word translated "church" literally means "the called out ones." The church is a community of "called out ones" — called out of the world's system into the communion of the saints. This "communion" is a close-knit, covenant community of believers who are all committed to the lordship of Jesus Christ and have become a part of His body. They love the Lord with all of their hearts, minds, and strength (Deuteronomy 6:4), and they love one another like Jesus loved them (John 13:34-35). As members of His body, His Church, being joined and held together by every supporting ligament, they grow and build themselves up in love, as each part does its work (Ephesians 4:16). God never intended for His people to live in the world and go to church, but rather to "live in the church and go to the world." One of the primary functions of this METRO is to prepare you to live in community.

The METRO uses the metaphor of a train stopping at several stations. Each station is a class or classes on a specific truth, principle, level of learning, or experience that will further equip you for leadership. Teaching the truth is a practice the Scriptures emphatically endorse. During His earthly ministry, Jesus spent much of His valuable time teaching (Matthew 9:35). He commissioned His disciples to teach (Matthew 28:20), and of course, we see in the book of Acts and in other epistles the apostles emphasizing the importance of teaching (Acts 5:25; 18:11; Colossians 1:28; 1 Timothy 4:6, 13; 6:3-4; Titus 2:7-8).

Historically, the benefit of teaching is rooted in the Old Testament. There is an anointing that is released in the world when the

Word of God is taught. The world desperately needs this anointing. When the Word is regularly taught to the people, calamities in society diminish. It is as though the Word forms an unseen barrier against which the evils of the world have little power." The light shines in the darkness and the darkness has not overcome it." (John 1:5 RSV)

At various points in Israel's history, the absence of a teaching priest (2 Chronicles 15:3) — one who taught the Word of God to the people (2 Chronicles 17:7) distinguished between the holy and the common, between the unclean and the clean (Leviticus 10:10-11) — opened the door for violence, great turmoil, and distress (2 Chronicles 15:5-6).

Teaching priests are still needed today; brethren who have spiritually qualified themselves by godly lifestyle to access God's presence (Psalm 24:3-6) and teach others. It is from the wisdom of a *teaching anointing* that these lessons are written. We hope this literary tool will be used to facilitate the entrance of many into spiritual maturity and fruitfulness.

Finally, as you board the METRO, stay focused on the destination. The METRO, like a natural train will stop at different stations along the way. Remind yourself that the stations are NOT your final destination. Stay focused. Get off the train at the various stations, experience the teaching of those stations, get your ticket punched, but get back on the train and go further. Continue until you have learned from all of the stations and achieved the destination of being equipped and mature. ALL ABOARD!

PREFACE

Grounding new believers in the Faith is one of the most important jobs of the local church. Many new converts do not continue walking with Christ because the church fails to ground them in basic truth. The new believer desperately needs the pure spiritual milk of the Word that he may grow (1 Peter 2:2). In the natural, no right thinking person would leave a newborn to survive on its own. Yet that is exactly what we do with newborn believers. They come to Christ one day and are left to their own devices the next. We expect them to learn how to feed themselves (read and obey the Word), wash themselves (confess their sins), and talk (pray) when they are only days old. The miracle is that, in spite of the church's lack of care, some survive. But even if we employed the most elementary follow-up materials available, the average local church could significantly increase the survival rate of new believers.

Mature believers have a two-fold responsibility: (1) to evangelize and follow-up those who are won; and (2) to disciple, by systematic teaching, those who are grounded. Notice these three levels of the work of the Church: evangelism, follow-up, and discipleship? By simple definition:

1) Evangelism is winning someone to Jesus Christ.
2) Follow-up is grounding him or her in the Faith.
3) Discipleship is teaching him or her how to win others and follow-up with them.

There is another level of the work of the Church called *multiplication*. By definition, multiplication is establishing the dominion of the kingdom of God through the strategic mentoring and oversight of those who are proficient in discipleship (level 3). In multiplication, ministry is actually multiplied to take territory. We must heed the call to occupy until He returns (Luke 19:13 KJV). We teach men, to teach men, to teach men. This produces spiritual productivity from one generation to the next.

A major goal is to establish in the hearts of men a world vision of God's dominion. It begins with the simple following up of the new believer with materials like these. Of course, our hope is that the new believer who becomes grounded in the Faith will get involved with other new believers, that this follow-up, maturing process might continue.

TABLE OF CONTENTS

1SALVATION ASSURANCE

What did I do to be saved?

You are saved when you do two things that

are outlined in the Scriptures:

Turn to God in repentance

Exercise faith in the Lord Jesus Christ.

1. WHAT DID I DO TO BE SAVED?

You are saved when you do two things that are outlined in the Scriptures:

a. **Turn to God in repentance** (Acts 17:30-31; 2 Corinthians 7:10), and

b. **Exercise faith in the Lord Jesus Christ.** (Romans 10:9-10)

The above two points were originally outlined by the Apostle Paul when he met with the Ephesian elders in Miletus:

> *I have declared to both Jews and Greeks that they must turn to God in repentance and have faith in our Lord Jesus.* (Acts 20:21)

Salvation is not a religion but a person: the Lord Jesus Christ. He is the only way to God (John 14:6). The Apostle Peter told the Sanhedrin Council,

> *Salvation is found in no one else, for there is no other name under heaven given to men by which we must be saved.* (Acts 4:12)

The assurance of salvation follows the obedience of the commands to repent and have faith (believe) in the shed blood of Jesus.

2. CAN YOU DEFINE THE ASSURANCE OF SALVATION?

The assurance of salvation is the inner witness from the Holy Spirit (Romans 8:16) when you have done what God commands. It means that you know that you have received what God has promised. God loves you and wants you to be assured of your relationship with Him. He does not want you to fear or doubt the reality of your salvation.

Even if He disciplines you, it is out of a love for you and desire for your growth and blessing. (Hebrews 12:5-7)

3. HOW DO I "TURN TO GOD IN REPENTANCE?"

To repent means to change. When you are sorry for sin (2 Corinthians 7:10), you determine, as an act of your will, to change your lifestyle, to change your behavior. Notice the Scripture,

> *Godly sorrow brings repentance that leads to salvation and leaves no regret, but worldly sorrow brings death.*
> (2 Corinthians 7:10)

Notice, godly sorrow is contrasted with worldly sorrow. The first produces life. It brings repentance that leads to salvation which leaves no regret. In other words, it creates change that results in deliverance, and that deliverance will fill you with joy and open you to faith and the blessings of God.

The second, worldly sorrow produces death. In other words, it gives a false sense of a relationship with God, when you are really separated from God. In worldly sorrow, you are probably sorry because you are caught in sin or its consequences, but you are not sorry enough to quit your sins and change.

On the outside, the two, *godly sorrow and worldly sorrow*, look the same, but the commitment to change is different. You will ultimately know the difference between the two by the results that are produced.

In summary, repentance includes asking God to forgive you for the wrong that you have done, and deciding to live a clean life. You cannot be saved without repentance.

The Scriptures plainly teach that God has commanded mankind to repent:

> *In the past God overlooked such ignorance, but now He commands all people everywhere to **repent**. For He has set a day when He will judge the world with justice by the man He has appointed. He has given proof of this to all men by raising Him from the dead.* (Acts 17:30-31)

Repentance is possible because God supplies you with the grace and strength to change. God would never command you to do something without giving you the strength and the grace to do it. Remember, to repent means to determine to change.

4. HOW DO I "EXERCISE FAITH IN THE LORD JESUS?"

You exercise or demonstrate that you have faith in the shed blood of the Lord Jesus Christ by doing three things:

a. Confess Jesus Christ as Lord, believing that He is risen from the dead

This means that, in prayer, you invite Jesus to come into your life and be your Lord. You then, **confess, or tell someone**, that you have yielded the control of your life to Jesus. Included in this, you believe with all your heart that Jesus is alive, risen from the dead, and that by virtue of His resurrection; Jesus is both Lord and Christ (Acts 2:32-36). When you do that, you are saved. Notice the Apostle Paul:

> *That if you confess with your mouth, "Jesus is Lord," and believe in your heart that God raised Him from the dead, you will be saved. For it is with your heart that you believe and are justified, and it is with your mouth that you confess and are saved.* (Romans 10:9-10)

The foundation for the salvation of mankind is the person and work of the Lord Jesus Christ (John 3:16). He is the Prophet (Hebrews 1:1-2), Priest (Hebrews 4:14-16) and King (Matthew 21:5) of your salvation. He came to guide, guard, and govern. As our prophet He came to guide us into the truth; as our Priest He stands in the presence of God, guarding our way into the presence of God, by way of His intercession and grace; and as our King He came to govern, to rule in our lives as our sovereign. He is the promised Jewish Messiah and the Son of the living God (Matthew 16:15-20). Jesus died on the cross of Calvary for your sins and rose from the dead that you might be saved (1 Corinthians 15:1-5). Your faith is in the person and work of the Lord Jesus on the cross of Calvary. Bible salvation cannot be found in any other (Acts 4:12).

b. **Praise and thank the Lord**

Clearly, **praise is faith in action**. When you praise the Lord after prayer, you are saying, "I believe that I have received what I requested." Therefore, by faith, you praise the Lord that you are now saved. Notice how important faith is in the Word:

> *And without faith it is impossible to please God, because anyone who comes to Him must believe that He exists and that He rewards those who earnestly seek Him.* (Hebrews 11:6)

You have earnestly sought the Lord by repentance and confession. Now, you praise and thank the Lord for saving you, because you believe that He has. God is pleased when we walk in faith, believing His Word. (Romans 10:17; 2 Corinthians 5:7)

c. **Receive water baptism.**

5. HOW IMPORTANT IS WATER BAPTISM?

Water baptism is very important. We are commanded in the Scriptures to be baptized. (Acts 2:38) Being baptized is the first thing you should do after repentance and faith. The order of the salvation events you must follow is: first, you repent of your sin; second, you exercise faith in Jesus by openly confessing Him as your Lord, believing that He is risen from the dead and, by faith, praising God for saving you; then third, you submit to the Christian ordinance of water baptism.

Then Peter said, "Can anyone keep these people from being baptized with water? They have received the Holy Spirit just as we have." So he ordered that they be baptized in the name of Jesus Christ. (Acts 10:46b-48a)

6. WHY IS BAPTISM CALLED AN ORDINANCE?

Baptism is called an ordinance because it has been ordered. You do not have an option. Your obedience to the lordship of Jesus Christ includes submission to the command, the order to be baptized.

7. WHAT WILL HAPPEN WHEN I AM BAPTIZED?

As soon as possible, after your conversion, the church will plan a baptism service. In preparation for your baptism:

a. You will attend a class on the Doctrine of Water Baptism.

b. You will publicly confess your faith in the lordship of Jesus Christ.

Then, in the presence of the congregation, in the name of the Lord Jesus Christ, the church will baptize you by immersion in a small pool designed for that purpose.

Peter replied, "Repent and be baptized, every one of you, in the name of Jesus Christ so that your sins may be forgiven. And you will receive the gift of the Holy Spirit. (Acts 2:38)

8. WHAT DOES BAPTISM MEAN TO ME AS A BELIEVER?

Baptism means that, by faith, you are identifying totally with the burial and resurrection of the Lord Jesus Christ. In baptism you are testifying to <u>God</u>, to <u>demons</u>, to the <u>world</u> and to <u>yourself</u> (a four-fold testimony), your obedience to this ordinance: "Jesus Christ is the Lord of my life, I am dead to the practice of sin and wrongdoing, and I am born again and have new life in Christ by faith."

In Him you were also circumcised, in the putting off of the sinful nature, not with a circumcision done by the hands of men but with the circumcision done by Christ, having been buried with Him in baptism and raised with Him through your faith in the power of God, who raised Him from the dead. (Colossians 2:11-12)

Baptism is more than simply "an outward sign or symbol of an inward work." Baptism is linked to our complete deliverance. The Old Testament Type of the Children of Israel being baptized by Moses in the Red Sea (1 Corinthians 10:2) includes baptism as a part of our complete deliverance.

By faith you have been freed from the bondage of sin to walk in the newness of life in Christ. Baptism is a confirmation of the genuineness of your living faith in the living Lord.

9. DOES BAPTISM SAVE ME?

No. You are saved because you repent of your sin and trust in the shed blood of the Lord Jesus Christ, making Him the

Lord of your life. It is the blood of Jesus that washes away your sins (Ephesians 1:7; 1 Peter 1:18-19; 1 John 1:7), not the waters of baptism.

The blood of the Passover lamb saved the children of Israel, not the waters of the Red Sea. The waters of the Red Sea showed them that they were, indeed, delivered by faith in God. In the same way, the waters of baptism confirm the genuineness of our faith in the shed blood of the Lamb of God, the Lord Jesus Christ.

For a more extensive doctrinal treatment of the truth of water baptism, read the book by the same author, <u>The Doctrine of Water Baptism</u>.

NOTES

2 DEVOTIONAL LIFE

WHAT IS PRAYER?

Prayer is communing with God.

Communing implies dialogue:

you talk to God and He talks to you.

1. WHAT IS PRAYER?

Prayer is communing with God. Communing implies dialogue: you talk to God and He talks to you.

2. DOES GOD ALWAYS HEAR ME WHEN I PRAY?

Yes. The Bible says that the eyes of the LORD are on the righteous and His ears are attentive to their cry (Psalm 34:15).

3. WHAT IS THE BEST TIME TO PRAY?

While it is true that we should always pray and not give up (Luke 18:1), the best time of day to set aside a special time to pray is early in the morning. Jesus prayed early in the morning:

> *Very early in the morning, while it was still dark, Jesus got up, left the house and went off to a solitary place, where He prayed.* (Mark 1:35)

4. WHAT SHOULD MY PRAYING INCLUDE?

In the Sermon on the Mount (Matthew 6:9-13), Jesus taught His disciples how to pray. His prayer outline includes three sections.

a. Worship: *"Our Father in heaven, hallowed be Your name..."* — You always begin with praise and worship to the Father because of who He is and what He has done. The psalmist taught that we enter His gates with thanksgiving, His courts with praise, and bless His *name* (Psalm 100:4).

b. Establishing Dominion: *"Your kingdom come, Your will be done on earth as it is in heaven..."* — Through fervent prayer, you establish the rule of the kingdom of God in your own life, in the lives of members of your family, in your local church, and in your local and national government.

This is taking dominion authority: the right and power to establish God's domain in the lives of men. Focus on praying for individuals that you know by name and by need in the following three areas:

Daily needs: "*Give us today our daily bread...*" — At this time, you specifically make your petitions known to God in faith with thanksgiving (Philippians 4:6-7). Remember that your request must be in the will of God, in other words, based upon a promise from the Word of God (1 John 5:14-15); must be specific (James 4:2b) as you ask with believing faith (Mark 11:24; James1: 6-8), and you must be prepared to tenaciously hold on with confidence (Galatians 6:9; Hebrews 10:35-39).

Reconciled relationships: "*Forgive us our debts, as we also have forgiven our debtors...*" — During this time you must examine yourself (2 Corinthians 13:5), determine to walk in daily confession and repentance (1 John 1:9) and determine to walk in forgiveness and reconciliation with all men (Matthew 6:14-15). After praying for yourself, you pray for those you are covering in the area of their interpersonal relationships. Pray that the grace to forgive and be reconciled dominates their relationships.

Will of God: "*And lead us not into temptation, but deliver us from the evil one.*" — During this time, you pray for the leading of the Lord in the lives of people you cover. The Lord wants to use you to pray against the temptation of the evil one whose purpose is to distract us from our purpose. When you pray for your brother, you open the door for the Lord to move in his life (even if he is not saved). You should pray for the Holy Spirit to guide your brother into fulfilling his destiny. Pray for him to put on the full armor of God (Ephesians 6:14-18) make the LORD his hiding and abiding place (Psalm 91:1, 9), for him to love the LORD with all of his heart (Psalm 91:14;

Deuteronomy 6:5), and to know the authority and power of His name (Psalm 91:14b; Philippians 2:9-11).

c. **Thanksgiving:** "*For Yours is the kingdom and the power and the glory forever, Amen.*" — As your prayer began with praise, it should end with you giving the Lord praise and thanksgiving. This conclusion reminds you of three things:

(1) The kingdom that is established is God's;

(2) The power that is needed to establish this kingdom comes from God (Zechariah 4:6; Acts 1:8);

(3) The glory and credit that will be given for what is established belongs ONLY to God. As you remember this, give the Lord praise at the conclusion of this special time of prayer.

5. WHAT IS WORSHIP?

Worship is your reverent spiritual response to the holiness and goodness of God. It should begin with joyful songs of praise (Psalm 100:1-2), but it is not limited to outward vocal expression. It can be inward and solemn. The Greek word for worship, proskuneo/προσκθνεο, means, "to crouch low; to prostrate yourself in homage or in reverence; to adore." True worship (John 4:23-24) is spiritual not physical. It may include outward joyful praise that takes on many forms from singing to dancing, and it is fulfilled as you experience the presence of God. The presence of God may be a humbling experience (Isaiah 6:5), and that is worship.

6. IS WORSHIP NECESSARY?

Absolutely! You will not become the mature, joyful believer God wants you to be without praise and worship. Worship is so vital; you are commanded to give unto the LORD the glory due unto His name and to worship the LORD in the beauty of holiness. (Psalm 96:7-9) Worship is warfare; it strengthens you to fight the good fight of faith.

7. HOW DO I WORSHIP THE LORD?

God is Spirit; therefore, you worship Him IN SPIRIT (by the Holy Spirit within you) and IN TRUTH (according to the Word of God) (John 4:23-24). It is essential to be filled with the Holy Spirit (Ephesians 5:18-19) and to know what the Word teaches about worship. You are exhorted to worship by the Spirit of God, to glory in Christ Jesus, and to have no confidence in the flesh (Philippians 3:3). This is a good beginning for entering into God's presence.

8. HOW DO I ENTER INTO GOD'S PRESENCE?

You come into the presence of God with praise. That is the key word — praise. The initial forms of praise are psalms (scripture put to music), hymns and spiritual songs. As the Spirit of God moves within you (Philippians 3:3), you express your love to God, adoring Him with all of your heart — allowing the fullness of your heart to be expressed with your lips (Psalm 100:1-2, 4; Colossians 3:16; Hebrews 2:12; 13:15).

9. WHAT ARE THE DIFFERENT EXPRESSIONS OF PRAISE TO GOD?

Your body is the greatest instrument of praise you have. Praise is full when it encompasses your mouth (voice), hands (arms), and feet (dance).

a. **Singing** (Psalm 9:2, 11; 59:16; 81:1)

b. **Audible praise** (Psalm 34:1; 103:1)

c. **Shouting** (Psalm 47:1; 63:1-3)

d. **Clapping** (Psalm 47:1)

e. **Dancing** (Psalm 149:3)

f. **Lifting hands** (Psalm 63:4; 134:2; 1 Timothy 2:8)

g. **Bowing, prostrating** (Psalm 95:6; Ezra 9:5)

h. **Musical instruments** (Psalm 150:3-5; Revelation 14:2)

10. HOW DOES GOD RECEIVE TRUE WORSHIP?

God loves true spiritual worship and is enthroned in the midst of it (Psalm 22:3). His dominion is manifested in you and in your circumstances as you praise Him. This can even, at times, produce an anointing in the atmosphere: a strong sense of His presence. Jesus said that the Father seeks true worship (John 4:23).

11. WHAT DOES TRUE WORSHIP DO FOR ME?

True worship will:

a. **Bring the revelation of God's presence and will.**
   (Isaiah 6:1-8; Acts 13:2)

b. **Create joy and strength in you.** (Psalm 46:4; Nehemiah 8:10)

c. **Establish the dominion of God in your life.** (Psalm 22:3)

12. WHAT DOES TRUE WORSHIP ENABLE ME TO DO?

True worship enables you to:

a. **Endure temptations and trials** (Matthew 24:13; James 1:12)

b. **Overcome sickness and disease** (Romans 8:2, 11)

c. **Witness with boldness and confidence** (Acts 4:31)

13. HOW DOES ALL OF THIS RELATE TO A DEVOTIONAL LIFE?

One of the most important disciplines that you need to place in your life is a consistent devotional life. When worship and prayer are practiced daily, you will greatly benefit. Most people refer to these types of devotions as — quiet time.

14. WHAT ARE THE STEPS TO A SUCCESSFUL QUIET TIME?

The real issue is consistency. It would be better to be consistent with a short quiet time, than to be inconsistent with a long one. The key is consistency. Notice the following steps in an average quiet time:

a. **Worship** — praising the Lord around His covenant names. Audibly exalting Him because of who He is and thanking Him because of what He has done and is doing.

b. **Confession** — boldly speaking forth the truth of the Word of God about who you are, what you have, and what you can do in Christ in the form of a prayer. For example, "Father, I thank You that I am blessed according to Your Word..."

c. **Wait** — pausing to listen in faith. Remember, prayer is dialogue.

d. **Requests** - these take on two forms and may need the use of a prayer list. Intercession is the first form — this is praying for others or standing in the gap for someone else. Petition is the second form — this is praying for your own needs in the name of Jesus. (Philippians 4:6-7)

e. **Study** - reading and studying the Word of God. Begin your Bible reading in the Gospels. Continue in the epistles; read the Psalms and Proverbs regularly.

f. **Meditation** - waiting in an attitude of worship and praise while thinking about the truths that you are spiritually digesting. You turn them over in your mind like you turn food over in your mouth as you chew it.

These are the basic guidelines that you will need to succeed in your devotional life. Though these are extensive, added to this list are a few further admonitions that you will need to succeed.

15. WHAT ARE THESE FURTHER ADMONITIONS?

a. **Set a time.** Make time to meet with the Lord. Sit down with your daily schedule and determine when you can get alone with God to pray and study the Word of God.

b. **Prepare a place.** Just like you have a place in your house to sleep, eat, watch television, etc., you need to choose a place for your quiet time, and get that place ready, sanctify it, for you to go there to pray and study the Word of God.

c. **Inform your friends.** The person(s) with whom you live should know the time that you meet God. They should be made aware of this special time of prayer and study. There may be many other times that you will be praying or reading the Word, but this time is a special time that

you have made an appointment with God. The purpose
in telling them is not to boast but to prepare them for
your absence during that season. The interruptions will
be less. In fact, it might be a good idea to even take the
phone off the hook during that time. Prayer and the
study of the Word of God should go uninterrupted.

16. WHAT IS MEANT BY THE PHRASE, "WORD OF GOD?"

The Word of God is the Bible, the 66 books of inspired
writings (Genesis - Revelation) also known as the Holy
Scriptures.

17. WHAT DO YOU MEAN, "INSPIRED WRITINGS?"

The Apostle Paul said,

> *All Scripture is God-breathed (inspired) and is useful for
> teaching, rebuking, correcting and training in righteousness,
> so that the man of God may be thoroughly equipped for
> every good work.* (2 Timothy 3:16)

The Scriptures are God-breathed, inspired, God spoken. This
means that the Scriptures have the authority of God Himself.
The 66 books of the Bible (Old and New Testaments) are the
Word of God.

18. WHAT ARE THE OLD AND NEW TESTAMENTS?

The Bible is divided into two main sections:

a. **The Old Testament**, the 39 books from Genesis to Malachi,
    covers the historical period from Creation to the Post-
    Exilic Period of Reconstruction (the time after the Jews
    returned to Canaan from captivity and began to rebuild).

b. **The New Testament** includes the 27 books from Matthew
to Revelation that deal with:

1) Matthew to John — The life of Jesus.
2) Acts — The history of the early church including
some of the ministry of the apostles Peter and Paul.
3) Romans to Revelation — Epistles (letters) from some
of the apostles to the early church.

19. WHERE SHOULD I BEGIN TO READ?

Begin reading your Bible in the New Testament. New converts
should first read the Gospels (Matthew to John) and learn
about the life of Jesus, the Messiah. Luke and Acts should
be read as one book since they are written by the same
author and cover the important history of the life of Christ
and the Early Church.

Next you should read and study the epistles because they
contain helpful exhortations (encouraging words that build
you up spiritually) from the first apostles to the Early Church.
Since you are a part of the Church, their exhortations are to
you as well.

You should regularly read through the Old Testament and
become familiar with its history and characters. Remember,
as you faithfully read the Word of God and the Lord blesses
and strengthens you, you need to begin to see yourself as a
student of the Word, one who is what we call "worded-up."

20. IS READING THE BIBLE ENOUGH TO BE STRONG IN THE WORD?

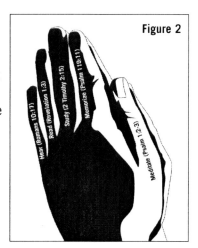

Figure 2

Reading the Bible is good, but just reading is not enough to gain a strong foundation in the Word. You need to be, as we often say, "Worded-up." To be worded-up, there are five things that you need to practice. These five things are a part of the Navigator's Hand Illustration (Figure 2).

a. **Hear** — You must make space in your life to consistently listen to the Word preached (worship services, Bible studies, television, and tapes) and sung (radio, gospel concerts, and tapes). Remember that faith comes by hearing the Word of God (Romans 10:17).

b. **Read** — You must set aside a time to read in the Scriptures systematically. You will be blessed if you do (Revelation 1:3).

c. **Study** — As you read, you should purchase other Bible study aides to assist you in learning the Word more thoroughly. Paul told Timothy to study (2 Timothy 2:15), and the Bereans were noted for searching the Scriptures thoroughly to confirm the truth (Acts 17:11).

d. **Memorize** — As you study, you will find that great benefit is derived from committing the Word to memory. The psalmist David called this, "Hiding the Word in your heart" (Psalm 119:11).

e. Meditate — This final area holds the other 4 together. The psalmist said that meditating upon the Word of God would make you like a tree: strong and fruitful (Psalm 1:2-3).

Practice all five consistently and the spiritual strength, maturity, and transformation that you experience will amaze you. There is no way to measure the blessing of being "Worded-up."

21. HOW IMPORTANT IS THE DISCIPLINE OF MEDITATION?

Before answering, let me say a word about meditation.

Hinduism has popularized meditation in the world. The World Book Encyclopedia says,

"Transcendental Meditation (TM) is a method of relaxing the body that became popular in the countries during the 1970's. It was developed in the 1950's by the Maharishi Mahesh Yogi, a Hindu monk from India. He used the word *transcendental* to describe the process of reaching a state of *pure consciousness*, where the mind is not aware of anything in particular. He declared that people who used this technique became happier and more relaxed and creative. People practice TM by sitting quietly in a comfortable position. They close their eyes and silently repeat their *mantra*, a pleasant-sounding word from the Hindu scriptures. Teachers of TM select a personal, secret mantra for each student. A person who practices TM meditates for 15 to 20 minutes in the morning or evening, before meals."

The mantra, the word that those who practice TM use to meditate, is usually the name of one of the many Hindu deities. Therefore, without knowing it, many that practice TM are secretly praying to one of the many false gods of Hinduism.

Christian meditation (CM) is the method of achieving spiritual strength and development through thinking about the truths of God and His Word. The Old Testament word **to meditate** (hagah) means to mutter; to imagine or think of; to speak quietly to yourself. Meditation is a spiritual discipline of the Christian Scriptures that is thousands of years old. *Meditation is a function of your heart, or your spirit man.* (Psalm 19:14) There are three areas of meditation that are taught in the Scriptures:

a. **The Word of God: its promises and truths** (Joshua 1:8; Psalm 1:2)

b. **The LORD Himself: who He is, His names** (Psalm 63:6; 104:34)

c. **The works of the LORD** (Psalm 77:12; 143:5).

Meditation is very important for a number of reasons:

a. **It is commanded.** Joshua 1:8 is a key passage on this truth of meditation. It teaches that rich blessings, or abilities, are attached to knowing and practicing the truth of meditation:

    The ability to obey — *"so that you may be careful to do everything written in it."* (Joshua 1:8b) Revelation for your practical Christian walk is received through meditation. The key emphasis in this regard is that through quiet disciplined speaking of the Word to yourself, you will receive understanding (revelation) that enables you to do what the Word says.

    The ability to prosper and be successful — *Then you will be prosperous and successful.* (Joshua 1:8c) Growth in stability, fruitfulness and personal prosperity is achieved through meditation. (cf. also Psalm 1:2-3)

b. **It produces inner spiritual strength** (Psalm 27:14; Isaiah 40:31). The discipline of meditation is a vital part of prayerfully waiting on the Lord.

22. WHAT TRANSLATION OF THE BIBLE SHOULD I USE?

You should purchase a modern speech version of the Bible. It can be either — The New International Version of the Bible (NIV), or The New King James Version of the Bible (NKJV).

Along with the help of the Holy Spirit (John 16:13), using a good modern speech version will help you achieve the correct interpretation of the Scriptures.

23. WHAT IS INTERPRETATION?

Interpretation is one of the three things that you must do to achieve Bible literacy and competence.

24. WHAT ARE THE THREE THINGS AND THEIR MEANING?

The three things are:

a. **Observation** — The discipline of looking closely at the truth and allowing it to speak to you. There are many things that you miss in your reading simply because you are not observant enough. Take your time, and look carefully. Ask yourself questions like: Who is writing? To whom is he writing? What is the subject matter? What are the main points? Why is he saying this?

b. **Interpretation** — This is the discipline of understanding what the text meant. Using the history of the author and the recipients, the meanings of the words he used, how the grammar affects the meaning, the contextual settings of the book and the passage, and the extended context of the teaching of that truth in other parts of the Scriptures, you ascertain the meaning of the text.

c. **Application** — The discipline of deciding what the text means to you. Included in this discipline is adjusting your behavior based upon your discoveries.

25. IS INTERPRETING THE SCRIPTURES NECESSARY?

Absolutely! Despite what some groups tell you, everyone interprets the Scriptures. Everyone! The question is — How well do you interpret? Don't be fooled. The Scriptures should be interpreted literally, grammatically, verbally and historically:

a. **Literally** — Most of the time, it means what it says and says what it means. Watch out for these people who always want to find some "deeper, hidden" meaning. Most of the texts of holy writ do not demand allegorical interpreting.

b. **Grammatically** — There are rules of grammar, which apply and should be used. Everything is not just up for grabs. There are rules!

c. **Verbally** — The words have meanings. These meanings must be looked up in the original languages. You will need a Bible Dictionary.

d. **Historically** — You must pay attention to the period of history during which the text was written. Can that history influence the meaning of the text? You'd better believe it!

26. ARE THERE OTHER BIBLE STUDY AIDES THAT I NEED?

Yes, there are four basic Bible study tools that you should buy:

a. **The New International Version of the Bible**

b. **The King James Version of the Bible**

c. **The Strong's Exhaustive Concordance of the Bible**

d. **W.E. Vine's, Expository Dictionary of New Testament Words.**

The above reference books are tied to the King James Version of the Bible (KJV). That is why the KJV is needed. It is also good to have because there are many great evangelists who still use it.

27. WHY IS HAVING A DEVOTIONAL LIFE SO IMPORTANT?

Because it is by being in the presence of God, and being judged and fed by the Word of God that we:

a. **Develop the character of God.** (Galatians 5:22-23)

b. **Reflect the glory of God.** (2 Corinthians 3:18)

c. **Conform to the likeness of Christ.** (Romans 8:29).

28. WHAT DOES IT MEAN TO DEVELOP THE CHARACTER OF GOD?

Developing the character of God is best achieved by abiding in the Vine, the Lord Jesus Christ (John 15:5), and yielding to the influence of the Holy Spirit (Ephesians 5:18). Manifesting the *fruit of the spirit* (Galatians 5:22-23) — love, joy, peace, patience, kindness, goodness, faithfulness, gentleness, and self-control — comes naturally as you discipline yourself in the abiding and yielding.

Jesus is the Vine and we are the branches (John 15:5). The fruit grows on the branches, in your born again, recreated human spirit, as you stay connected to the Vine. To develop in this fruit of the spirit is to develop the character of God in you. Try not to confuse the fruit of the spirit (Galatians 5) with the gifts of the Spirit (1 Corinthians 12). The first you *grow* in, the second you *flow* in. The fruit represents character that must be developed by you with the Spirit's help; the gifts represent manifestations that come upon you in your availability, as the Spirit wills (1 Corinthians 12:11).

Remember, the key is — *abiding* in the Vine, and *yielding* to the Holy Spirit.

> *I am the Vine; you are the branches. If a man remains in Me and I in him, he will bear much fruit; apart from Me you can do nothing.* (John 15:5)

> *Do not get drunk on wine, which leads to debauchery. Instead, be filled with the Spirit.* (Ephesians 5:18)

> *But the fruit of the Spirit is love, joy, peace, patience, kindness, goodness, faithfulness, gentleness and self-control. Against such things there is no law.* (Galatians 5:22-23)

29. WHAT DOES IT MEAN TO REFLECT THE GLORY OF GOD?

To reflect the glory of God is to mirror His purpose and will in all that you do (1 Corinthians 10:31). Your reflection of His glory is strongest when you are abiding in His presence. Paul taught that you are even transformed more and more into His image, from glory to glory, by His Spirit as you spend time in His presence:

> *And we, who with unveiled faces all reflect the Lord's glory, are being transformed into His likeness with ever-increasing*

glory, which comes from the Lord, who is the Spirit.
(2 Corinthians 3:18)

30. WHAT DOES IT MEAN TO CONFORM TO THE LIKENESS OF CHRIST?

To conform to the likeness of Christ is to do everything to the glory of God (John 17:4), and to be a servant (Philippians 2:5-8). Jesus sent His disciples forth with the commission, "As the Father has sent Me, so send I you." (John 20:21) As you do as He did, as you die to yourself so that others might live in Him (John 12:24), the kingdom of God will be established with power.

For those God foreknew He also predestined to be conformed to the likeness of His son, that He might be the firstborn among many brothers. (Romans 8:29)

NOTES

3 THE BAPTISM WITH THE HOLY SPIRIT

The phrase "Baptism with the Holy Spirit" is used by Jesus (Acts 1:5) to reference the promise the Father made to pour out His Spirit upon all flesh (Joel 2:28).

1. WHAT IS THE BAPTISM WITH THE HOLY SPIRIT?

The phrase "Baptism with the Holy Spirit" is used by Jesus
(Acts 1:5) to reference the promise the Father made to pour
out His Spirit upon all flesh (Joel 2:28). With this baptism,
believers are endued with power from God for the purpose of
performing ministry. There are different terms or phrases used
in the Bible to reference this experience (Luke 24:49). It is
called an anointing, a baptism, being clothed with power, an
infilling, and an outpouring. All these phrases refer to the
same experience that provides power to believers for effective
witnessing (Acts 1:8). The following are different references
to this same experience:

> "*I baptize you with water for repentance. But after Me will
> come one who is more powerful than I, whose sandals I
> am not fit to carry. He will baptize you with the Holy Spirit
> and with fire.*" (Matthew 3:11)

> "*The Spirit of the Lord is on me because He has anointed
> me to preach good news to the poor.*" (Luke 4:18)

> "*I am going to send you what My Father has promised;
> but stay in the city until you have been clothed with power
> from on high.*" (Luke 24:49)

> "*But you will receive power when the Holy Spirit comes
> on you; and you will be my witnesses in Jerusalem, and
> in all Judea and Samaria, and to the ends of the earth.*"
> (Acts 1:8)

> "*All of them were filled with the Holy Spirit and began to
> speak in other tongues as the Spirit enabled them.*"
> (Acts 2:4)

> "*When they arrived, they prayed for them that they might
> receive the Holy Spirit, because the Holy Spirit had not yet*

come upon any of them; they had simply been baptized into the name of the Lord Jesus." (Acts 8:15-16)

"*While Peter was still speaking these words, the Holy Spirit came on all who heard the message. The circumcised believers who had come with Peter were astonished that the gift of the Holy Spirit had been poured out even on the Gentiles.*" (Acts 10:44-45)

All the above scriptures refer to the one experience that Jesus said is, "what My Father has promised" (Luke 24:49), and that Peter said was the fulfillment of the Father's promise given through the prophet Joel, "*In the last days, God says, I will pour out My Spirit on all people. Your sons and daughters will prophesy, your young men will see visions, your old men will dream dreams. Even on my servants, both men and women, I will pour out My Spirit in those days, and they will prophesy.*" (Acts 2:17-18)

Peter is actually quoting from the prophecy of Joel:

"*And afterward, I will pour out My Spirit on all people. Your sons and daughters will prophesy, your old men will dream dreams, your young men will see visions. Even on my servants, both men and women, I will pour out My Spirit in those days.*" (Joel 2:28-29)

2. WHO BAPTIZES WITH THE HOLY SPIRIT?

Jesus is the One who baptizes believers with the Holy Spirit according to the words of John the Baptist in Matthew 3:11. (See previous reference: Joel 2:28-29)

3. **ARE THERE ANY REQUIREMENTS I MUST MEET TO RECEIVE THIS EXPERIENCE?**

Yes, there is one requirement. To be filled with the Holy Spirit, you must be a believer. Jesus said that the world cannot receive the Holy Spirit (John 14:17), and the apostles said that the Holy Spirit is given to those who obey Him (Acts 5:32). Therefore, you must obey God and believe to receive the Holy Spirit.

4. **WHY IS THIS EXPERIENCE NECESSARY?**

This experience is necessary for two reasons:

a. **Power** — You need the power that Jesus promised (Acts 1:8). He told His disciples to wait for this power. Therefore, it must be necessary.

b. **Prayer** — When you receive the Holy Spirit as they did in the Acts of the Apostles, with the initial manifestation of speaking in other tongues, that gift of tongues assists you in prayer and worship. It is important for you to receive this assistance at the very beginning of your Christian experience. Speaking in tongues is the only gift of the Spirit (1 Corinthians 12) connected with prayer. Because of the importance of prayer, you can see why the Lord gives this initial manifestation of the Spirit's presence in the life of the new believer. You cannot survive spiritually without prayer. In His wisdom, God has given you His Spirit to help you.

5. **WHAT EXACTLY IS THE SPEAKING WITH OTHER TONGUES?**

To speak in tongues is to speak a language that you have not studied or learned. God supernaturally gives it to you when you receive the gift of the Holy Spirit (Acts 10:44-46).

We are told in the historical account (Acts 2:3-4) that tongues of fire came to rest on each of them and ALL of the 120 believers in the upper room were filled with the Holy Spirit and began to speak with OTHER tongues. There are five accounts in the book of Acts where persons received an initial baptism with the Holy Spirit. In every account, tongues is either specifically stated or implied in the events of the narrative.

The pattern is set for believing how the Holy Spirit will be received in Acts 2:3-4. ALL received and ALL spoke in OTHER tongues. If the Lord wanted you to believe that the speaking with other tongues is not for every believer, He needed only to baptize some of the initial 120 in the upper room of Acts 2 without them speaking in other tongues. But it states specifically that they all spoke in OTHER tongues; not the same tongues but OTHER tongues[1]. The word "other" is in the original text. They ALL spoke in OTHER tongues.

The apostle Peter and the brethren who had come with him knew that Cornelius and his household received the Holy Spirit when they heard them speaking with tongues (Acts 10:45-46). If that is how they knew then, that is how we know today.

6. HOW CAN I BE FILLED WITH THE HOLY SPIRIT?

Any born again believer can follow these simple steps and be filled with the Holy Spirit:

a. **Understand that, if you believe on the Lord Jesus Christ and are saved, you received the Holy Spirit by virtue of being born of the Spirit** (John 3:5-8; Romans 8:9). Being born of the Spirit is not being filled with the Spirit, but please know that you do have the Holy Spirit in your life.

b. **Understand that God has promised to fill you with His Holy Spirit. God has not changed. The promise is valid** (Acts 2:38-39).

c. **Simply ask the Father to fill you with the Holy Spirit** (Luke 11:13).

d. **By faith, open your mouth, and breathe in the wind of the Holy Spirit.** Rejoice that God keeps all of His promises, and that you are filled according to His Word. Since you are a child of God, you qualify for the Holy Spirit. You believe God's promise and believe He wants to fill you, and so you have asked in simple faith.

e. **Now, in faith, open your mouth and begin to speak the words that the Spirit gives you.** *You* must speak and give the Holy Spirit a voice. Since you cannot speak two languages at once, stop praising the Lord in English and begin to praise Him in the language the Spirit gives you. The Spirit will not force you to speak. You can lift up your voice and utter those sounds that you hear in your spirit.

f. **Continue to speak out even those utterances and phrases until a full flow comes.** Remember, tongues is a language not jibberish. Do not settle for jibberish. Expect to speak a language that the Spirit gives you (Acts 2:4).

g. **Finally, remember that in the name of Jesus, you can speak in the Spirit** (in other tongues) (Mark 16:17), and that the speaking is done by you. The Spirit does not speak in tongues, you do. He only gives you the utterances, but you do the speaking.

7. HOW CAN I STAY FILLED WITH THE HOLY SPIRIT?

Here are some guidelines you can follow:

a. **Walk in** —

Repentance — Walking in the discipline of repentance is to continually determine to change as an act of your will. To repent means to change your mind, to be transformed because your mind is renewed by your total commitment to the Lord and His Word (Romans 12:1-2). It includes pressing toward the goal to win the prize for which God has called you heavenward in Christ Jesus (Philippians 3:13-14). The goal, of course, is establishing God's kingdom in you and in your world.

Submission — Walking in submission means you daily surrender your will to God (James 4:7). You walk in humility by submitting to your brethren in Christ (Ephesians 5:21) and by submitting to the spiritual authority of your church leaders (Hebrews 13:7, 17).

b. **Worship** — Yield yourself daily to the influence of the Holy Spirit (Romans 6:13; 12:1-2; Ephesians 6:10-18) by spending time praising and worshiping the Lord in the Spirit (John 4:23-24; Ephesians 5:18-19).

Howard Carter, former general supervisor of the Assemblies of God in Great Britain, and founder of the oldest Pentecostal Bible school in the world said this: "Speaking with other tongues is not only the initial evidence of the Holy Spirit's infilling, but it is a continual experience for the rest of one's life to assist you in the worship of God. Speaking in tongues is a flowing stream which should never dry up, but should enrich your life spiritually." Brother Carter's statement is a good statement, even though, theologically speaking, tongues should not be referred to as the evidence of the Holy Spirit's infilling. A better statement is, "Tongues is a manifestation of the Holy Spirit that every Spirit-filled believer has a right to expect."

c. **Work** — Staying filled with the Holy Spirit will take making yourself a conduit through whom the Spirit can flow.

   1) In prayer, take dominion over your circumstances by verbally standing upon the Word (Proverbs 4:20-22). Speak to your mountains, those difficult circumstances confronting you, in the name of the Lord Jesus Christ (Mark 11:23; John 14:14) and rejoice in the Lord always (Psalm 34:1; Philippians 4:4).

   2) Boldly confess Christ to men (Matthew 10:32), and testify of God's goodness (Psalm 107:2).

   3) Position yourself to share the good news of salvation through Christ to all that will listen (Matthew 28:19; Romans 1:16-17), and let your light shine (Matthew 5:14-16; Isaiah 60:1-3; 2 Corinthians 4:3-4).

Staying filled with the Baptism with the Holy Spirit needs to be understood in connection with other baptisms in Scripture.

8. WHAT ARE THE OTHER BAPTISMS WE NEED TO UNDERSTAND?

There are actually four baptisms that exist today, including the one taught in this chapter. A part of you being grounded in Christ is understanding the meanings of these different baptisms. The four baptisms are:

1. The baptism of believers into the Body of Christ — In this baptism, the Holy Spirit places believers into the Church, the Body of Christ, when they are born of the Spirit (John 3:5; 4:14; 1 Corinthians 12:13).

2. The baptism (immersion) of believers in water — In this baptism, a mature believer[2] completely immerses the believer in a body of water, in the name of the Lord. This water baptism is also called Christian Baptism. (Matthew 28:19; Acts 2:38; Romans 6:3-9; Colossians 2:12)

3. The baptism of believers with the Holy Spirit — (Acts 2:1-4) In this baptism, the believer receives power for ministry (Acts 1:8). Through the Old Testament prophet, God promised to pour His Spirit upon us (Joel 2:28). Jesus confirmed the promise (Luke 24:49; Acts 1:4-5); the Apostle Peter confirmed that the spiritual outpouring on the day of Pentecost was the fulfillment of the promise (Acts 2:14-18). According to John the Baptist, Jesus baptizes believers with the Holy Spirit (Matthew 3:11), but Jesus said that you could ask the Father for the Holy Spirit (Luke 11:13). Actually, the Holy Spirit is seen as being sent by the Father and the Son (John 14:26; 15:26).

4. The baptism of suffering — Through this baptism, the believer is prepared for more effective ministry. Jesus mentioned this baptism to His disciples (Mark 10:38-39). This baptism was the path Jesus walked. A pattern of ministry moves those who desire to be used, to follow the Jesus path. This is the path of resurrection through crucifixion. Paul talked of knowing Christ in the power of His resurrection and in the fellowship of His sufferings (Philippians 3:10).This same path is seen in other passages. The account of Israel in the wilderness means that through the pressure of suffering and struggle victory appears. Complaining only delays the promotion process. Complaining also closes the door of understanding. You cannot move on until you learn the lesson your trial is teaching. It is as if God keeps bringing you back to the same trial until you pass it with praise.

Murmuring delays maturation. God made the Captain of your salvation perfect through suffering (Hebrews 2:10). You point men to Him because of the pathway He created through the blood of His Cross. When you suffer for righteousness, i.e. for the establishment of righteousness in the earth (John 16:10), you actually make it easier for others to hear you. Jesus is seen in us and our message is more palatable because of the brokenness created through suffering. Paul said death is at work in us but life is at work in you (2 Corinthians 4:8-12). The one who God uses will suffer in order to produce the life of God in others. This process is a part of the pattern seen in ages past, and most poignantly through the person and work of Christ (John 12:24).

One of the baptisms is called an ordinance, a practice that is ordered by the Lord. It is the ordinance of Water Baptism, number two. There is another ordinance practiced regularly in the local church.

9. WHAT IS THAT OTHER ORDINANCE?

It is the ordinance of The Lord's Supper: a covenant meal instituted by the Lord Jesus on the eve of the Passover before His crucifixion.

10. WHY DO WE PRACTICE THIS OBSERVANCE?

The Lord's Supper is a sacred observance where believers have a covenant meal together where the Lord is present. The grace of healing (spiritual, emotional, and physical) accompanies this observance along with the benefit of reconciliation when it is practiced properly.

When you partake of the Lord's Supper together, you are saying three important things:

1. I am in covenant with you (Proverbs 18:24).

2. I love and trust you as my covenant brother or sister (Proverbs 17:17).

3. I will be loyal to you (Proverbs 27:6).

Finally, the clear exhortation of the apostle Paul in 1 Corinthians 11:29-30 is that to eat the Lord's Supper without recognizing the binding elements of covenant and without responding to your covenant responsibilities is to eat and drink the Lord's judgment on yourself. In the church at Corinth, some were weak spiritually, some were sick physically, and some had even died prematurely ("fallen asleep") because of this covenant offense.

---

[1] Some want to believe that since all who spoke in tongues on the Day of Pentecost were Galileans (Acts 2:7) and since Judea is listed in the roll call of nations (Acts 2:9), then some of the 120 did not speak in "other" tongues, since historically Galileans and Judeans spoke the same language. But remember, the text said that they were all filled with the Holy Spirit, and began to speak with other tongues, as the Spirit enabled them. Evidently, the dwellers from Judea (Acts 2:9) who were in Jerusalem on the day of Pentecost, spoke another language than the Galileans. But of course that must be true, for why would they be surprised to hear the wonderful works of God spoken by those who normally speak their own language? The miracle was that they heard those who they knew did not speak their language, speaking their language.

[2] Some would contend that only an ordained or licensed minister of the Gospel should baptize a new believer. While I see merit in not permitting just anyone to administer baptism, Scripture teaches that mature laymen baptized believers (Acts 9:10, 18).

NOTES

NOTES

4OVERCOMING TEMPTATION

Temptation is the act of being enticed

to do something that is forbidden by the

Word of God. The prime example is the

temptation of Adam and Eve in the

Garden of Eden.

1. WHAT IS TEMPTATION?

Temptation is the act of being enticed to do something that is forbidden by the Word of God. The prime example is the temptation of Adam and Eve in the Garden of Eden. God strictly forbade them to eat or touch the fruit of the Tree of the Knowledge of Good and Evil, but they disobeyed the commandment of the Lord, yielded to the temptation and ate (Genesis 3).

2. HOW DOES TEMPTATION TAKE PLACE?

James outlines the stages of the development of temptation,

> *But each one is tempted when, by his own evil desire, he is dragged away and enticed. Then, after desire has conceived, it gives birth to sin; and sin, when it is full-grown, gives birth to death.* (James 1:14-15)

You can clearly distinguish three stages in the process of temptation:

a. *"But each one is tempted when, by his own evil desire, he is dragged away and enticed."* This is where temptation begins. The sin is not in being tempted. Even Jesus was tempted. The sin is in yielding to the temptation. This beginning stage is when you are enticed. An evil desire, one in which you have not judged yourself, can drag you away and entice you.

b. *"Then, after desire has conceived, it gives birth to sin."* After you are enticed, you yield to commit an act of disobedience. Yielding to the temptation is where the sin is actually committed. The seed began to sprout in the desire of your own mind, but the seed does not take root until you act upon that desire.

c. *"and sin, when it is full-grown, gives birth to death."*
Spiritual death or separation from God does not take place
immediately after the sin is actually committed. You first
lose fellowship with God (1 John 1:6). Then, if the failure
is not judged and repented of, and you continue to
practice that sin, it will grow and separate you from God
(Romans 6:23).

3. SHOULD I EXPECT TO HAVE VICTORY OVER TEMPTATION?

Yes indeed! Paul wrote to the Corinthians:

*No temptation has seized you except what is common to
man. And God is faithful; He will not let you be tempted
beyond what you can bear. But when you are tempted,
He will also provide a way out so that you can stand up
under it.* (1 Corinthians 10:13)

Praise the Lord! God has promised to provide a way out
of defeat during temptation. You can stand up under the
temptation and experience the blessing of victory.

4. WHAT HAPPENS IF I FAIL?

If you fail, you are not lost. God has made provision for
your failure. John wrote in his first epistle,

*My dear children, I write this to you so that you will not sin.
But if anybody does sin, we have One who speaks to the
Father in our defense — Jesus Christ, the Righteous One.
He is the atoning sacrifice for our sins, and not only for ours
but also for the sins of the whole world.* (1 John 2:1-2)

John exhorts you in verse 1 not to sin. He also encouraged
you that God has made provision for you in Jesus Christ
the Righteous One, if you do sin. Jesus is your advocate
who is in the presence of the Father to speak on your behalf.

He is like your lawyer in the Father's courtroom. Thank the Lord for this abundant provision.

Therefore, if you fail in any way, all you need to do is confess that failure to the Father, in the name of Jesus, and He will forgive and cleanse you (1 John 1:9). Being restored from broken fellowship because of sin is just that simple. Simply confess the failure to the Father.

5. HOW DO I CONFESS MY SINS?

John wrote in his first epistle:

> *If we confess our sins, He is faithful and just and will forgive us our sins and purify us from all unrighteousness.*
> (1 John 1:9)

To confess your sins means to acknowledge, to God, the wrong that you have committed. Of course, God already knows what you have done (Psalm 139:1-4), but your honest acknowledgement of your wrongdoing is the first step toward forgiveness and deliverance. The Proverbs tell us how important honest acknowledgement is to your being delivered:

> *He who conceals his sins does not prosper, but whoever confesses and renounces them finds mercy.*
> (Proverbs 28:13)

The key to being forgiven and freed from the bondage of sin and wrongdoing is to openly confess it and thoroughly renounce it to God. He promised to forgive and cleanse you. Do not try to conceal it, confess it. To conceal or hide your sin only makes it worse, but to confess it and turn from its practice, opens the door for genuine deliverance.

6. DO I HAVE TO CONFESS TO MEN?

According to 1 John 1:9 (see page 48) and other parallel passages, the principle is that our sins should be confessed to God who promises to "forgive and purify us." Confessing sins to a man, minister, or priest is not necessary. Only God can forgive us, so we are to confess our sins to God.

But we should not be afraid to acknowledge what we were (before we were saved). Paul evidently knew, through their own testimonies, the past sins of some of the Corinthians,

> *Do you not know that the wicked will not inherit the kingdom of God? Do not be deceived: Neither the sexually immoral nor idolaters nor adulterers nor male prostitutes nor homosexual offenders nor thieves nor the greedy nor drunkards nor slanders nor swindlers will inherit the kingdom of God. And that is what some of you were. But you were washed, you were sanctified, you were justified in the name of the Lord Jesus Christ and by the Spirit of our God.*
> (1 Corinthians 6:9-11)

Remember that we overcome the enemy by the "blood of the Lamb and by the word of our testimony." (Revelation 12:11) Powerful things take place in you when you boldly testify about your deliverance. We do not brag on our past, but we should not be afraid to share, as a witness, what we were before we met Christ.

7. IS IT EVER NECESSARY TO CONFESS TO SOMEONE?

There is a spiritual principle that says — "*You should confess a sin as far as it is known.*" The principle is based upon the teaching of Jesus in the Sermon on the Mount,

> *Therefore, if you are offering your gift at the altar and there remember that your brother has something against you,*

*leave your gift there in front of the altar. First go and be
reconciled to your brother; then come and offer your gift.*
(Matthew 5:23-24)

In other words, if, in my transgression, I have wronged another
person in some way, it is not enough for me to confess only
to God. I must also confess to that person or persons as well.
Maintaining reconciled covenant relationships is very important
for continued spiritual growth and development.

For example, suppose someone has an argument with his wife
and in anger he says some unkind words that hurt and offend
her. After being convicted by the Holy Spirit, he must repent
to God (confess, acknowledge his wrongdoing to God),
AND he must confess to his wife as well. His repentance
is incomplete without the second part. In doing both, he is
released and delivered from the guilt and bondage of the
failure. Public confession, if practiced biblically, can
strengthen the deliverance process and keep unclean
spirits from gaining ground in your life (Ephesians 4:27).

8. CAN A BELIEVER HAVE AN UNCLEAN SPIRIT?

It is possible for a believer to have an unclean spirit. This is
not a matter of demon possession. Demons do not possess;
they do not own you and cannot own you. The Lord owns you
(1 Corinthians 6:19-20). But demons can control areas of
your life if you yield to their influence (Ephesians 4:27).
If a believer continues to yield to the influence of a demon
spirit, he or she can gradually lose control of their life in
that area.

9. WHAT MUST HE DO TO GET FREE?

If a believer finds that he has lost control of his or her life in a particular area, he may need deliverance. He may need to have the demon cast out of him. The general discipline of counting yourself dead to a sin (see page 53, question 14, letter b) should be applied first, but if it fails, another approach is open to him. Know this my friend — if the presence of a demon spirit is causing the problem, counting yourself dead to the sin is not enough. You can count yourself dead to a simple lust of the flesh (Galatians 5:19-21) and gain the victory, but you cannot count a demon dead, because they will not die and you cannot kill them. No, they must be driven out of your life.

10. HOW CAN I DRIVE OUT A DEMON?

You command the demon to leave in the name of Jesus Christ (Luke 10:17-19; Mark 16:17; Acts 16:18). You may not be able to do it yourself, therefore, get two other strong believers to help you.

11. IS IT POSSIBLE TO FALL AWAY FROM THE FAITH?

This is not a question that needs to concern you. While it is possible to fall away from the Faith, falling away from the Lord is no easy matter. God's love is great and His mercy eternal.

You must understand this: one does not lose his salvation in the process of struggling with sin. It is only after the struggle ceases and the will to fight dies that the creeping death of apostasy begins. Then the understanding can again become darkened and the heart hardened to the things of God (Ephesians 4:18). None of this takes place overnight. The Scriptures teach that it is a gradual process (James 1:14-15).

Take heed. To be forewarned is to be forearmed. Remember, God is on your side. It is His perfect will for you to prosper spiritually. Fear not!

12. WHAT IS THE DIFFERENCE BETWEEN FALLING INTO A SIN AND THE PRACTICE OF A SIN?

There is a great difference. Of course it is true that "all have sinned and fall short of the glory of God" (Romans 3:23), but failing in an area and repenting of that failure, cannot be compared with the decision to practice a sin.

The first is the normal course that the believer takes to restore the broken fellowship that happens after sin. He confesses his sin and receives forgiveness and cleansing (1 John 1:9).

The second is not normal. It occurs either with a believer who is on the verge of apostasy (2 Peter 2:14-15) or with someone who has never been saved (1 John 3:5-8). The Apostle John taught that to practice sinning is to either:

a. **Sin unto death** (1 John 5:16), or to

b. **Never have been born of God** (1 John 3:9).

13. HOW CAN I KEEP FROM FALLING INTO SIN?

You will need a good foundation if you hope to survive the storms of life (Matthew 7:24-27). The beginning of a solid foundation for maturity is the discipline of obedience. I repeat — *The Discipline of Obedience*. For now, my friend, follow the six steps to victorious living.

14. WHAT ARE THE SIX STEPS TO VICTORIOUS LIVING?

Here are six steps you can take to assure victory:

a. **Faithfully fulfill all of the initial salvation steps that are set forth in the Scriptures** — Repentance, Faith and Water Baptism (Acts 20:21; Mark 16:16).

b. **Count yourself dead to sin but alive to God in Jesus Christ** — Determine not to let sin rule you and dominate your mortal body. Determine not to give yourself and the members of your body as instruments of sin, but yield yourself to God (Romans 6:11-14).

c. **Set aside a special time and place to daily read the Word, memorize edifying Scripture passages, meditate and pray** (Jeremiah 15:16; Psalm 119:11; 1:2; 1 Thessalonians 5:17).

d. **Break worldly ties and determine to spend more time with believers, not only on Sundays but during the week** (2 Corinthians 6:17-18).

e. **Boldly confess to both family and friends that Jesus Christ is now your Lord** (Matthew 10:32-33).

f. **Walk as a little child** (Matthew 18:1-4).

15. WHAT DOES IT MEAN TO WALK AS A LITTLE CHILD?

It means to live your life in a child-like manner. Note "child-like" does not mean "childish." There is a difference. Jesus said,

> *At that time the disciples came to Jesus and asked, "Who is the greatest in the kingdom of heaven?" He called a little child and had him stand among them. And He said, "I tell*

you the truth, unless you change and become like little children, you will never enter the kingdom of heaven. Therefore, whoever humbles himself like this child is the greatest in the kingdom of heaven. (Matthew 18:1-4)

Notice three major characteristics of a little child:

a. Loving — a child is quick to love and accept.

b. Trusting — a child is quick to trust and believe.

c. Forgiving — a child is quick to forgive and reconcile.

All of us are familiar with negative "grown-up" behavior. Though we are accustomed to the unloving, suspicious, grudge-holding ways of the average adult, even within the Household of Faith, we must come to recognize that God requires a quality of character and integrity in us, that the world does not have.

The normal characteristics of a little child best illustrate the kind of behavior you should seek to exemplify.

16. ARE THERE SOME INSTITUTIONAL PITFALLS I SHOULD AVOID?

Yes! One of the common mistakes many believers make is NOT recognizing the danger of association with "secret societies." These are organizations that use secret rituals or ceremonies to bring in new members. This is usually called "pledging" during which candidates are required to undergo a period of indoctrination where they take an oath of some sort including a prohibition against divulging the rituals and ceremonies of the pledging process to outsiders.

Fraternities, sororities, and lodges comprise the secret societies you are most likely to encounter. Freemasonry is one of the worst, and while it is true that these organizations provide some valuable community service, you cannot overlook the mixture of Christianity, the occult, and eastern religions in the oaths and rituals new members are required to undergo. Be careful and unyoke yourself (2 Corinthians 6:14-16).

17. HOW DO I GET OUT OF THE SOCIETY THAT I BELONG TO?

You should be able to leave the secret society by writing a letter of resignation to both the local chapter and the national office. It would be a good idea to include in your letter some of the scriptural objections to the ceremonies and rituals in which you participated.

18. HOW DO I RELATE TO OTHER SOCIETY MEMBERS ONCE I LEAVE?

As believers we must always remember God loved the world enough to send His Son to die for it (John 3:16). God demonstrated His love for sinners (Romans 5:8) and wants to save them (1 Timothy 1:15). Therefore, it is important that your attitude towards former secret society colleagues is one of love and humility. Don't condemn them for remaining in the society, and don't use your leaving as a club with which to beat them. Simply point them to the scriptures as an explanation for your decision to leave and remember to pray for the salvation of those who are lost. Trust God to open the eyes of those who are saved but yet choose to remain.

NOTES

NOTES

5STEWARDSHIP

Tithing is one of those local church

disciplines few practice with consistency.

A common excuse is, "I will tithe when

I get a 'real' job making some 'serious'

money." But the sad truth is that "he

who is faithful over little will be faithful

over much, and he who is unfaithful over

little will also be unfaithful over much."

(Luke 16:10)

INTRODUCTION

Tithing is one of those local church disciplines few practice with consistency. A common excuse is, "I will tithe when I get a 'real' job making some 'serious' money." But the sad truth is that "he who is faithful over little will be faithful over much, and he who is unfaithful over little will also be unfaithful over much." (Luke 16:10) The principle is you must show yourself faithful over the little before you can have responsibility over the much.

The pastor of an affluent congregation once said, "If everyone in my congregation was on welfare and simply tithed the ten percent as God's Word commands, the income of the church would triple." Obviously, most of his people did not start tithing after they got the "real" job. What about you? What excuses are you giving for ignoring God's Word about tithing?

You may ask the question, "How do I begin?" The answer is simple — start where you are; e.g. tithe from your allowance; tithe from your welfare check; tithe from your after school part-time job. Prove faithful over the little and one day you will have responsibility over the much. What you learn from the patterns practiced in the early development years significantly shapes your perspective and influence your decisions later on. In tithing language, honoring God with the first fruits of your increase (Proverbs 3:9) as a young person in your teens and twenties, prepares you to walk in the benefit of that honor within all the areas of your life including family, finances, and future. In essence, it is receiving the long-term benefits that accompany faithfulness.

Frequently asked questions like — "Why should I tithe to the church? Can't I just give to needy people on my own? Can the church be trusted with my tithe?" — indicate an underlying distrust many have with the church concerning money. No doubt the genesis of the complaint was the financial scandals surrounding television ministries of the past, like PTL. Tens of thousands of believers donated multiplied millions of dollars, prompted by the charisma of a televangelist. Obviously, it is not possible to know the character of a man from long distance. It takes watching a pastor's life, knowing his family, and witnessing his leadership in the handling of money and ministry before you can determine whether he is a shepherd or a hireling. That's why your tithe should be given in the local church. You can deal with the issue of distrust by witnessing the character of ministry in the local church with your own eyes, and the work of the ministry will not be hindered by the disobedient withholding of your tithing dollars.

It goes without saying that money is important to most Americans. As a culture, we treat it as a status indicator, a security blanket, and for some — money is like a god. Christians are not exempt from money's influence, and if we are not careful, even mature believers may make giving decisions based on the economy. To put in proper perspective the influence money can have on us, Jesus taught that no one can serve both God and money (Matthew 6:24). You can only have one master. He who is ruled by God will not be ruled by money and vice-versa. You must ask yourself, "Where is your heart?" Jesus said that you could tell where someone's heart is by where he spends his money (Matthew 6:21). Don't let the pattern of this world influence you, but renew your mind with the truth of God's Word and be transformed (Romans 12:2). Your mind can be renewed, restored, and revived away from the general financial distrust of ministry when the Word of God is obeyed (Psalm 19:7-9) and when you take the time to look carefully at the local ministry under which you sit.

But while the general financial distrust of ministries may have some basis in fact, there can never be a valid excuse for withholding your resources from God's work. This does not mean you should give blindly; give responsibly, check ministries out. Excellent ministries will provide financial reports. But even apart from that, you should give where you are fed spiritually and where you are led to give by God. Don't allow man's unfaithfulness and corruption cloud God's faithfulness to you. You are called to seek first His kingdom and His righteousness. This includes making your resources available to the kingdom.

Is tithing a legalistic part of the Law of the Old Testament? Shouldn't we give from our hearts, or out of a sense of being led by God? Unfortunately, too often this is just another way of saying, "I give when I want to." In fact, those who love money more than they love God's kingdom seldom feel "led" to give. They hear the voice of their hearts to spend money on themselves instead of giving to God's kingdom. But what about the legalistic aspect of tithing... isn't tithing apart of the Old Testament Law that was fulfilled in Christ?

Well technically, tithing predates the Law. Abraham paid tithes to Melchizedek more than 400 years before the Law came through Moses (Genesis 14:17-20; Hebrews 7:1-11). Through Melchizedek, God blessed Abraham, and he then gave Melchizedek a tithe of everything. Incidentally, Abraham became one of the wealthiest men of his day. Do you see a connection to giving and prosperity? The Bible does!

Let's take a second look at tithing. God is generous by nature and wants you to be like Him. Be like God and be a giver. God so loved the world that He gave (John 3:16). The Old Testament pattern is that giving is a tool for receiving. Even though you may not live in an agricultural area, yet the principle of seedtime and harvest, sowing and reaping still works. Truth in principles was applicable in ancient times and is applicable today. Let the following Old Testament references help you examine how God directed Israel to serve Him through giving and how they prospered:

  a. **The Consecration of the Firstborn** (Exodus 13; Nehemiah 10-36)

  b. **The Feast of Harvest or First Fruits** (Exodus 23:16,19; Leviticus 23:10,17; Deuteronomy 26:1-15)

c. **The Gleaning Privileges** (Leviticus 19:9-10, 23:22; Deuteronomy 24:19-22)

d. **The Sabbath Rests** (Exodus 23:10-11, 12; Deuteronomy 5:12-15; Mark 2:27-28)

e. **The Year of Jubilee** (Leviticus 25:8-55)

f. **Tithing** (Leviticus 27:30; Genesis 14:20; Deuteronomy 12:17, 26:1-15 especially vs. 12; Numbers 18:21; Malachi 3:6-12)

The New Testament teaches tithing also, but on some occasions the giving goes beyond a tenth. There's the story of the widow giving all she had to a corrupt temple, and yet Jesus calls her blessed (Mark 12:41-44). This should help those who feel compelled to examine and question different expenditures in the budget before paying their tithes. Paul's exhortation to Christians in one city to help the needy in another (2 Corinthians 8-9) goes on to say that you will reap what you sow; if you sow a little you reap a little and if you sow a lot you reap a lot (2 Corinthians 9:6), and that God loves a cheerful giver (2 Corinthians 9:7). Again remember the admonition of Jesus that where your treasure is your heart will also be (Matthew 6:21).

Finally, there are some things connected to tithing and giving you need to know. Money has such a pervasive power in our culture that you must confront it on many fronts. To successfully adopt a godly view of money and possessions, you need to change your view of success and your perception of worth. You need to understand the implications of being a part of a different kingdom and the importance of *feeling* and knowing you are a part of that kingdom. There is security in the will of God; God's presence is in His will. He promised to never leave you or forsake you (Hebrews 13:5). This is especially true when you do His will (Matthew 29:19-20). In the process of being content, you are encouraged to wear the world like a loose garment and not to love things (1 John 2:15-16). Remember you brought nothing into this world and you will certainly take nothing out (Job 1:21). Therefore, be a good steward of your possessions because you really do NOT own anything; you can only use things. Therefore, use things and love people, not visa versa, and you will find yourself inexorably drawn into the benefit of the will of God. This is actually a pattern that when developed and practiced will enrich your life and also position you to touch the lives of others. Allow yourself the privilege of being His hands extended. Let us not become weary in doing good, for at the proper time we will reap a harvest if we do not give up (Galatians 6:9).

1. WHAT IS STEWARDSHIP?

Stewardship is concerned with more than just finances but with all of life. It recognized that one day you will stand before the judgment seat of Jesus Christ and give an account for the deeds you have done in the body, whether they are good or bad (2 Corinthians 5:10). The "deeds" include the management of all your life resources: physical health, relationships, physical possessions, time, talent, and financial possessions. The subject of *stewardship* embraces all of life, and God is calling you to be a good steward.

2. WHAT IS A STEWARD?

In the New Testament, a steward (Greek: oikonomos/οικονομο) is a manager, usually the manager of a household, one trusted with responsibilities and who is under authority. A steward is a manager of another's property.

3. WHAT IS THE MAIN RESPONSIBILITY OF A STEWARD?

The main responsibility of the steward is *faithfulness*. He is to be faithful in his walk, his talk, and in the discharging of his responsibilities. Faithfulness requires a readiness to obey, to pray, to submit, and to discipline one's self. The New Testament pictures Christians as stewards.

Moreover it is required in stewards, that a man be found ***faithful***. (1 Corinthians 4:2 KJV)

4. WHAT ARE THE SPECIFIC AREAS IN WHICH I SHOULD BE FAITHFUL?

You are to be faithful in three specific areas:

a. **The discipline of your time** (Ephesians 5:16). This includes church attendance, Bible study, prayer, and Christian fellowship.

b. **The use of your natural talents and spiritual gifts for the strengthening of brethren in the church** (1 Corinthians 12; Ephesians 4:16).

c. **The giving of tithes and offerings from your financial resources to support God's work** (Malachi 3:8-11; 2 Corinthians 9:6-11).

5. WHAT IS BEING A GOOD STEWARD OVER MY FINANCIAL RESOURCES?

First, it means you faithfully pay your **tithes** to the Lord. Jesus taught you can detect where a man's heart is by where his treasure (money) is (Matthew 6:21). People of the world spend hundreds and even thousands of dollars weekly on drugs and gambling because that is where their hearts are. When the Lord truly has your heart, He will also have your tithe. The Bible teaches that the tithes belong to the Lord (Leviticus 27:30; Deuteronomy 12:11; Malachi 3:8-10).

For where your treasure is, there your heart will be also. (Matthew 6:21)

Second, it means you understand the **tithe** connects you to God's covenant. Paying your tithes qualifies you to participate in the covenant benefits of prosperity and protection. Adam and Eve enjoyed all the benefits of covenant living with God when they walked in obedience, but when they ate of the tree of the knowledge of good and evil, they were ejected from Eden.

The tree of the knowledge of good and evil belonged to the Lord, just like the tithe belongs to the Lord. Therefore, eating of the tree is tantamount to believers taking God's tithe and eating it. Many are ejected from God's covenant blessings because they have touched and eaten God's tithe (Genesis 3:1-24). Achan did the same. He took from the tithe, the first-fruit-city of the land, the goods from the city of Jericho, after the LORD told them that all the goods of Jericho belonged to Him (Joshua 6:18-19; 7). A sign should be put over the tithe, "Do not eat; do not touch; this belongs to God." Taking from God's tithe disconnected these brethren from the benefits of the covenant. Taking from God's tithe disconnects brethren today from the full benefits of the covenant.

6. DOES THIS DISCONNECTION MEAN A LOSS OF ETERNAL REDEMPTION?

No. Paradoxically, you are saved by grace through faith and not by works (Ephesians 2:8-9). The paradox is that while works do not save you in eternity, works are important for the salvation-sanctification experience of time. You are created in Christ to perform good works which God has foreordained that you should walk in (Ephesians 2:10). Paying your tithes is a work that benefits you NOW during your earthly pilgrimage. While it is true that there will be those in heaven who did not tithe, the full benefits of the covenant God reserves for His faithful people in the earth. And an integral part of their faithfulness is tithing.

7. WHAT IS A TITHE?

The word tithe literally means "tenth." To give your tithe is
to give the first tenth of your income to the work of the kingdom
of God. Practically speaking, it means if you gross $100.00
in your pay, your tithe would be the first $10.00. Let me
repeat, the tithe is the first tenth. Most believers who tithe
do not pay the first tenth but somewhere near the last. The
tithe is first fruits — the first tenth.

Tithing is God's means of supporting the work of His kingdom.
All do not give the same amount, but all give the same
percentage — a tithe (the first 10%). The pastor of a large
affluent church was quoted as having said, "If all of my
people were on welfare but paid their tithes, our church's
income would triple."

8. WHERE IS TITHING TAUGHT IN THE BIBLE?

a. Tithing is taught in the Old Testament. Here are some
key passages:

Genesis 14:19-20 — teaches Abram gave tithes to
Melchizedek (who prefigured Christ, see Hebrews 7:1-17).

Leviticus 27:30 — teaches the tithe is holy and belongs
to the LORD.

Nehemiah 10:37 — teaches the tithes belong to the
Levites (priests); i.e. the tithes are used to support those
who are in full time ministry.

Malachi 3:8-11 — teaches to withhold your tithes is to
rob God and put yourself under a curse, but when you
tithe God open the floodgates of heaven to bless you
immeasurably and rebuke the devourer (the enemy: insect,
human, or demon) on your behalf.

*Will a man rob God? Yet you rob Me. But you ask, "How do
we rob you?" In tithes and offerings. You are under a curse
— the whole nation of you — because you are robbing Me.
Bring the whole tithe into the storehouse... Test Me in this,
says the LORD Almighty, and see if I will not throw open the
floodgates of heaven and pour out so much blessing that
you will not have room enough for it. I will prevent pests
from devouring your corps,* (Malachi 3:8-11)

b. **Tithing is taught in the New Testament.** Here are some
key passages:

Matthew 23:23 — Jesus rebuked the Scribes and
Pharisees for their hypocrisy. They paid tithes but
neglected the weightier matters of the law: justice,
mercy and faithfulness. He commended them for their
tithing when He said, "You should have practiced the
latter without neglecting the former."

Luke 6:38; 2 Corinthians 9:6-11 — teach giving is
connected to sowing and reaping, a principle of
prosperity in the kingdom.

1 Corinthians 16:2 — teaches your giving is "percentage
giving" (as in the Old Testament), in keeping with your
income.

Hebrews 7:1-10 — teaches that Melchizedek, if not the
pre-incarnate Christ, is a type of Christ, and when Abraham
paid tithes to Melchizedek, it represents the faith children
of Abraham (Galatians 3:26-29) paying tithes to Christ
(His Church). Christ is a priest forever according to the
order of Melchizedek (Hebrews 7:17) and we are a
part of the seed of Abraham by our faith in Christ
(Galatians 3:26-29).

Clearly, tithing is taught in the Bible, Old and New Testaments, and the benefits of tithing are seen in Bible history: provision, prosperity, and protection. The song poet exclaims, "You can't beat God giving, no matter how you try." Giving begins with the tithe. As one of my mentors, Rev. Ernest G. Billingsley, would say, "Tithing is the lowest branch upon which the Christian chicken can roost." Amen!

9. WHAT ABOUT OFFERINGS?

By definition, offerings are the gifts you give above your tithes. You can also rob the LORD by withholding offerings (Malachi 3:8). The offering indicates your commitment to sacrificially support the work of the kingdom. Jesus commended sacrificial giving (Mark 12:41-44). Remember, you actually pay your tithes, pay because it is like a bill that you owe — the tithe belongs to God; it is not yours to keep. But you give an offering willingly out of the love of your heart. When you give an offering, you sow a seed expecting to reap a harvest. Notice these four laws of the harvest:

a. **You reap if you sow** — reaping requires sowing; you cannot expect to reap a harvest of any kind if you do not sow any seed.

b. **You reap what you sow** — the DNA for reaping is in the DNA of the seed you sow. Apple seeds produce apple trees from which you reap apples. Someone once said, "Any fool can count how many seeds are in an apple, but no man can count how many apples are in a seed."

c. **You reap after you sow** — in the order of progression: sowing must precede reaping; you must recognize the commodity in the equation called "time." Also, the gestation period of the seed, the time it takes for the seed to mature to reproduce, must be taken into account in the expectation of a harvest.

d. **You reap more than you sow** — one apple seed produces one apple tree that after maturity produces apples every year. Each of those apples contains seeds. Again, it's been said, "Any fool can count the number of seeds in an apple, but no one can count the number of apples in a seed." Reaping more than you sow also reminds us of the words of Edwin Louis Cole, "You can gain by giving what you cannot buy with money."

Finally, take note of the following passages that exhort giving,

> *Give, and it will be given to you. A good measure, pressed down, shaken together and running over, will be poured unto your lap. For with the measure you use, it will be measured to you.* (Luke 6:38)

The abundance of the harvest is indicated by the words "good measure, pressed down, shaken together and running over." It is the picture of an overflowing barrel of flour that is a good measure, pressed down, shaken together. Flour has a tendency to fill with air giving a false sense of fullness, but in this picture, the flour in the barrel has been shaken together and pressed down to remove the air. Therefore, the overflowing barrel is really full. God desires your finances to reflect this picture. The act that initiates this is GIVING, and the beginning of giving is tithing.

> *Remember this: Whoever sows sparingly will also reap sparingly, and whoever sows generously will also reap generously.* (2 Corinthians 9:6)

> *One man gives freely, yet gains even more; another withholds unduly, but comes to poverty.* (Proverbs 11:24)

Giving to God's work is never negative, always positive. You cannot out-give God. Giving to God's work always produces blessing and prosperity in you. God has ordained it. When you give to God, you sow seed that sets in motion the laws of the harvest. You must reap. Giving opens the window of increase in your life. You may not see the increase today or tomorrow, but as sure as God is alive and you are faithful, increase and prosperity will come upon you and overtake you (Deuteronomy 28: 1-2).

Therefore, do not be weary in well doing (Galatians 6:9), cheerfully follow the command to sow your financial seed into God's soil (2 Corinthians 9:7), and you will surely reap a great harvest (Matthew 19:29).

10. IS GOD CONCERNED ABOUT MY FINANCES?

Most assuredly yes. Jesus taught more about money than about heaven or hell. He said, "You cannot serve both God and money." (Matthew 6:24) You must love and serve God, but only use money. Do not love or serve money; use it to do the work of the kingdom. God expects you to be a good steward. Do you remember the parable of the talents? A *talent* was a measure of money in Bible times. In the parable, Jesus commends the stewards who used their master's money profitably (Matthew 25:20-23). Are you using, in a profitable way, the resources God gives you?

God has the right by creation (Psalm 100:3) and redemption (Isaiah 43:1) to require your cooperation in the building of His kingdom. You belong to the Lord; you are NOT your own (1 Corinthians 6:19-20). It is in God you live, move, and exist (Acts 17:28). As your creator, He instructs you how to live your life, and since money is such an important part of life, His instructions include how you should spend your money. This not only includes paying your tithes, but also how you spend the remaining 90%. The way you relate to and handle money largely determines how much the Lord can use you.

11. WHY DOESN'T EVERYONE IN THE CHURCH TITHE?

Everyone does NOT tithe for several reasons:

a. **Some are NOT saved**; they attend church and may give
    something, but because they do not know the Lord, they
    walk according to their own desires and do not tithe.
    (Cf. 1 Corinthians 2:14)

b. **Some call themselves saved, but have not made a total
    commitment of their lives to the lordship of Jesus Christ.**
    They are not submitted to the authority of the Word or
    the delegated authority of the pastors. Therefore, they
    walk in disobedience to God's tithing mandate. Their
    salvation is questionable.

c. **Some are saved but are misinformed about God's tithing
    mandate.** They believe that tithing is not for today, but
    was only for the saints in the Old Testament. They may
    be good givers, but will fall short of faithfully tithing.
    Unfortunately, these will be excluded from the benefits
    tithing brings.

d. **Some are saved and believe in God's tithing mandate to the
    church, but because they have problems with the leadership
    or with the direction in which they see the church going,
    they feel they have the right to withhold their tithes.** But
    Jesus commended the widow for giving everything she
    had to a temple run by corrupt leaders (Mark 12:41-44).
    You cannot use your disagreement with the church's
    leadership as an excuse for not tithing. If you disagree
    that much, leave. Put yourself under leadership you trust
    and pay your tithes there. If you stay, pay your tithes.

e. **Some are saved members of the church, they believe in God's tithing mandate, but because of the unwise handling of their money, their indebtedness precludes their being able to faithfully tithe.** These need to give and talk with their pastors about budget counseling and the existing debt cancellation programs.

f. **Some are saved members of the church, but they feel that because these are tough times economically, they cannot afford to tithe.** But the very opposite is true: they cannot afford not to tithe.

12. WHAT IS THE ANSWER TO THESE "NON-TITHING" DILEMMAS?

The only answer to rebellion and disobedience is repentance. If you are not paying your tithes, you are guilty of stealing and must repent. As a pastor, I have often thought, "What would it be like if all the believers actually believed, took God at His Word, and faithfully paid their tithes?" Our annual tithing budget would grow 3 to 5 times its present amount. Local churches could purchase their own neighborhoods, provide for the homeless and indigent, and develop economically without the need for bank assistance. In fact, the church could own a bank. Oh the good God's people could do if their energy and time were not wasted on motivating people to give. Oh the programs God's people could finance if the church's money is not wasted on paying the interest from borrowed money. You must learn how to give in faith. Let me say again, if you do not have confidence in the leadership of your church, or in the direction it is going, you should NOT withhold your tithes. If you cannot in good conscience give your money there, you should find another church and become an active, giving part of that assembly.

Also, if you want to tithe but feel you cannot, an important solution is creating a budget. There are counselors to help you. By all means, get out of debt, especially credit card debt. Ask for help. There are financial counselors positioned and ready to assist you. We need you to be the best believer God wants you to be.

13. WHAT PART DOES SUBMISSION TO AUTHORITY PLAY?

Submission to authority plays an important part in your deliverance and prosperity. You were delivered from the bondage of sin because you submitted to the authority of the Word of God, called on the name of the Lord, and were saved (Romans 10:13). You acted in faith based upon your belief of the truth. You believed, submitted to the authority of the truth you believed, acted, and the faith accompanying that truth supported and strengthened you to be saved. That is it in a nutshell.

The same way submission to authority works for deliverance, it works for prosperity. According to the truth of the Scriptures, prosperity is connected to sowing or giving. Jesus said if you give you receive an abundant overflow from others (Luke 6:38).

Real submission to authority is you seeing yourself as one who is under authority. This principle releases blessing in every area of your life. The story of the centurion illustrates how being "under authority" releases strength to operate with authority and revelation to see others who are "under authority" (Matthew 8:5-13). The centurion's definition of who he was and how he saw himself was, "I also am a man under authority" (Matthew 8:9), (those under authority eventually become persons with authority). Then the centurion described the level of authority in which he operated, "with soldiers under me; and I say to this one, 'Go!' and he goes, and to another 'Come!' and he comes, and to my slave, 'Do this!' and he does it." Most want the benefit of commanding others without the responsibility of obeying the one over them.

The centurion also recognized by revelation the authority of Jesus' words. There must be something about being under authority with others under you that enable you to understand the power of words. The centurion knew his superior's words were powerful in his own life, and he knew his words were powerful in the lives of those under him. He could then recognize the power of the words of Jesus and asked him, "Just say the word, and my servant will be healed" (Matthew 8:8).

When submission to authority exists with all of the respect and honor intact, doors of revelation and power open causing a release of blessing, healing, strength, and financial resources. If the saints could just look beyond what they see in the natural, operate by faith and give out of obedience to the authority of the Word, they would be blessed beyond all they can ask or think.

14. WHAT DO THE SAINTS NEED TO FAITHFULLY PAY THEIR TITHES?

The saints need to understand several important truths about tithing:

a. **Tithing is not an option; the tithe belongs to God** (Leviticus 27:30).

b. **Tithing says you see God as your source and you are trusting that He will faithfully keep His promises** (Malachi 3:10-11).

c. **Tithing is a covenant connector.** Giving your tithes and offerings says you are connected to the covenant of provision in the kingdom. This means that God is establishing His kingdom through the financial strength of believers. When you faithfully tithe and give offerings, you connect yourself with what is close to the heart of God — His kingdom coming. Your tithing will connect you to God's covenant of prosperity: i.e., He will be obligated to keep you healthy and working so that your provision will not cease. (Cf. 2 Corinthians 9:6-9)

d. **Tithing is a seed that will produce prosperity in those who sow in faith** (Proverbs 3:9-10; Luke 6:38). It is a mistake to think you will get ahead financially by NOT giving (Proverbs 11:24).

One man gives freely, yet gains even more; Another withholds unduly, but comes to poverty. (Proverbs 11:24)

And God is able to make all grace abound to you, so that always having all sufficiency in everything, you may have an abundance for every good deed. (2 Corinthians 9:8)

Any fool can count how many seeds there are in an apple, but no man is wise enough to count how many apples there are in a seed.

You can gain by giving what you cannot buy with money. (Edwin Louis Cole)

NOTES

6 A DOCTRINAL STATEMENT

The teachings of this ministry follow the

fundamental truths of Christian orthodoxy

outlined in the following statements:

G.A. Thompson

The teachings of this ministry follow the fundamental truths of Christian orthodoxy outlined in the following statements:

1) We believe that the Scriptures, Old and New Testaments, are God-breathed: that by the supernatural influence of the Holy Spirit, the biblical writers wrote the divine, trustworthy, and authoritative Word of God, the only rule of faith and practice (Matthew 5:18; 24:35; 2 Timothy 3:16; 2 Peter 1:20-21).

2) We believe in the one true God who has revealed Himself as eternally existing in three persons: Father, Son, and Holy Spirit; distinguishable yet indivisible (Deuteronomy 6:4; Matthew 28:19; Luke 3:21-22; 2 Corinthians 13:14).

3) We believe in the Incarnation: the deity of Jesus of Nazareth — that He is Lord, the Son of the living God, was conceived by the Holy Spirit, born of the virgin Mary, and is truly God and truly man (Luke 1:26-35; John 1:1, 14, 18; Isaiah 7:14; 9:6; Philippians 2:5-11; Revelation 1:7-8; 22:12-13, 16).

4) We believe that mankind was originally created by God in His image, fell into sin through disobedience, marred God's image, plunged all of creation into depravity, and made it impossible for man to save himself (Genesis 1:27; 3; Romans 5:12).

5) We believe in the Substitutionary Atonement: that Jesus, the Christ died on the Cross for our sins, obtained eternal redemption for us, was buried, and was raised bodily from the dead on the third day, fulfilling Old Testament prophecy, and appeared to His disciples (Isaiah 53; Luke 24:1-3; Acts 1:1-3; 2:22-36; 1 Corinthians 15:1-8; Hebrews 9:12-14).

6) We believe that Jesus of Nazareth ascended bodily into heaven, was exalted to the right hand of the Father, and that He will literally and physically return the second time for the Church (John 14:2-3; Acts 1:9-11; Philippians 2:9-11; 1 Thessalonians 4:13-5:11; Hebrews 9:28).

7) We believe that the personal salvation of the repentant sinner, by grace through faith in the finished work of Christ on the Cross, produces the "Abundant Life" (Isaiah 53:4-5; Matthew 8:16-17; John 10:10; 19:30; Acts 17:30-31; Romans 5:1-2; Ephesians 2:8-9; 1 Peter 2:24).

8) We believe in water baptism by immersion, as an obedient response of the believer to the command of the Lord (Matthew 28:19; Acts 2:38; 19:1-5).

9) We believe in the baptism with the Holy Spirit, the promise of the Father for empowering believers to witness about Christ (Luke 24:49; Acts 1:4-8; 2:1-4).

10) We believe that speaking in other tongues is an initial manifestation of the Baptism with the Holy Spirit that every believer has a right to expect, and that the charismatic gifts of the Holy Spirit are to operate in the local church until Jesus returns (Acts 2:4; 10:44-46; 19:6; Romans 12:6-8; 1 Corinthians 12:8-10; Ephesians 4:11).

11) We believe in the local church as the primary instrument of God in the earth to disciple men, and to establish the kingdom of God through prayer, fellowship, and the ministry of the Word (Matthew 28:19-20; Acts 2:42-47; 6:4; 20:28; Ephesians 4:11-16; 2 Timothy 2:2; Hebrews 10:25).

12) We believe that on the "Last Day," Jesus will return in the "Second Coming," there will be a resurrection of the dead including the righteous and the wicked, and after judgment the righteous will be rewarded, but the wicked will be punished (Daniel 12:2; John 5:28-29; 6:39, 40, 44, 54; 11:24; Acts 24:15; 1 Corinthians 15:51-52; 1 Thessalonians 4:16-5:11; Revelation 20:11-15; cf. also Matthew 25:31-46).

NOTES